The mathematics of love

Sonia Hunt

The mathematics of love

Acknowledgements

My thanks to the members of the Wednesday Evening Poetry Group at NSW Writers Centre Rozelle for sharing the art and friendship of poetry.

Many, many thanks to Norman Neill, convenor of the Poetry Group, for his invaluable critique and generosity.

Particular thanks to Colleen Keating and John Egan.

Thank you to Simon for his patience and typesetting.

My loving appreciation to David for providing me with a model of the not-so-Pure Mathematician and for inspiring the title *The mathematics of love*.

Thank you to Sarah in Geneva for providing me with a perfect photo of Cleopatra as she relieves the existential boredom of existence by strolling down her back lane in Arzier.

The mathematics of love
ISBN 978 1 76109 051 6
Copyright © Sonia Hunt 2021
Cover image: Gerd Altmann from Pixabay

First published 2021 by
Ginninderra Press
PO Box 3461 Port Adelaide 5015
www.ginninderrapress.com.au

To Vera with love
1928–2019

Contents

Berry Love
Mathematics in love	13
Berry love	14
So romantic	16
Muse	18
An orange for you	19

Migraine à trois
Migraine and sexy feet	23
Migraine is not sexy	25
I am penitent	26

On Night
Fox Valley dreaming	29
Fox Valley night	30
Leura night	31
Leura moon	32
Swinging in the rain	33

Font
This my Jug	37
I give you flowers	38
The Fairest Font	39
Guest house	40
Romance	42

Pentagon
Man of flowers	47
Teddy bear	48
Package	49
The unkindest cut	51
Lens	52

Circumstantial
    Ode to a daughter   55
    The wait   56
    Wisp   57
    The art of passion   58
    The art of simplicity   59
    Time for bed   61

Gradient of Love
    Agapanthus Triptych   65
    Lyric   67
    Still life   68
    Adoration on a Silent night   69

Sunburnt Country
    Sunburnt Country   71

Poetica
    To My Coy Mistress   79

Finis
    Saying it   85

Notes   87

This morning over the weir the diver bird drank
and the kookaburra sang with a full beak of dawn

Berry Love

Do I repeat myself, of course I do!

Mathematics in love

On my 43rd birthday
and six weeks before
my Statistics in Psychology exam
you told me
that I was the most naturally
non-mathematical person
you had ever met
and you wrung your hands
when I confused the symbols
'less than' and 'greater than'.

Your coaching was sheer talent.

On my 53rd birthday
you rushed downstairs
excitedly clutching a poem
you had written as a surprise:
'my little wife
is the trial and trouble
of my life'.
I chortled with pleasure.

My favourite memory
is when you booked
an expensive restaurant
to celebrate our thirty-three
and a third wedding anniversary.

Only a mathematician
could be such a romantic.

Berry love
(after WCW)

(i)

I'm having some strawberries
I said to you
they are so juicy and sweet:
later for me, you said.
Did you know that the riddle
of life's meaning could reside
in the flesh of a humble berry:
I held it up to the light.
Each one is actually an ovary
with the olfactory capability
of provoking
an hedonic response within us.
The Functions of Complex Variables
provoke a hedonic response in me
you muttered.
I popped the strawberry
into my mouth
savouring its bright pigment
and swallowed it philosophically.

(ii)

You know how much
I enjoyed the roast chicken
last night you said,
and I know
you were planning to give
the leftovers
to the adorable Bosie and Cheetah.

Well, I have a confession:
when I was making coffee
this morning
I opened the fridge
and noticed the chopped chicken
in a bowl
tightly covered in cling wrap
beside the punnet of strawberries.

I was reminded
of how delicious the chicken had been,
I'm afraid I have eaten most of it.

On the other hand
if you had leapt
out of bed a little earlier
you might possibly
have restrained me.

So romantic

By way of conversation
I asked if you could suggest
a metaphor
for our road trip.

Two white lines
running to infinity
you said. By the way,
I've made a calculation:
tomorrow is the 48th anniversary
of the day we met
so don't tell me I haven't got
a romantic bone in my body.

That first dance
wasn't it 'Strangers in the night'
I mused:
I remember how the room rocked
salty with swaying bodies
the girls' skirts a swish
of fluted pirouette
and the music, so romantic
in the semi-darkness
caught between passion and entreaty.

Do I repeat myself
of course I do!

Later that night
trying to get comfortable
I shifted your awkwardly placed hand
from my abdomen
and pulled down the moon
that was shining through the window
under the covers.

Muse

My husband told me
to stop scribbling
in my notebook
and bloody well enjoy
the view of the Hunter
which was after all the reason
we were holidaying there.

I told him
I had grown up
watching bloody gum trees
whizzing past car windows
and in my view
their view
hadn't got any better.

That night we drove
through dark country roads
to a restaurant in a farm house.
As we pulled up
I could see the word MUSE
imprinted on a wall
in elegant cursive.

I was gobsmacked
and we had a lovely evening.

An orange for you

I wanted to show you
how an orange is peeled
but I was stopped
by its bite on my tongue.

I wanted to show you
its marmalade colour
so I swivelled its thick skin
between my fingers.

I wanted to squeeze
its sweet zest for you
to swallow but you said
it was too sticky.

Then I told you
to close your eyes
as I slipped a sliver of orange
from my mouth into yours
and you moaned slightly.

And swallowed it without fuss.

Migraine à trois

One poem about migraine could be considered a misfortune,
but three begins to look like carelessness!

Migraine and sexy feet

Bearing a migraine is an art
a form of suffering I have honed
over years of practice.
Perhaps a Rembrandt could paint me
in this pose my robe in a dangle
over a prostrate body
the back of a hand strategically placed
upon my forehead
eyes prettily fluttering with each throb.

My feet are exposed
in this master's painting
arched in a fetching stretch
of homage to the sun.
They are I think the best
part of my anatomy
an expression of my minority
Chinese genes.
I coyly admit I have often
admired them myself.

Once as a teacher-librarian
I was standing on a stool
to reach a top shelf for stocktaking
when the Maths master wandered in
and to my surprise stood so close to me
that looking down I could see
the sparse crown of his head.
We were both silent as he seemed to gaze
hypnotised before my bare feet.

Then he cleared his throat
and said with deliberation sotto voce
that my feet were the sexiest
he had ever seen.
My Maths master (for I now felt some degree of
the proprietorial towards him) departed, leaving
behind him a little rainbow of smiles
that I filed under the Dewey number
for Originality.

And somehow I think
that is about the closest
I will ever get to being the subject
of a true Master.

Migraine is not sexy

I am prostrate on the sofa
fingernails deep in my temple
conscious of the pot belly burning
the masks on the wall
their eyeless faces contorting
into the weeping
of Picasso's Dora.

I am counting hard
eyes shut tight
panting between hot spits of wood
I feel Dora's pain;
relief comes slowly
into veins that dilate
between synaptic points of

Yes! Yes!

Amazing Grace!

Migraine is a lot like childbirth:
you really don't want
to be there.

I am penitent

I am crouching
on the sofa
feet arched in pain
one eye tortured
by the caprice of light;
clutching an icepack
I sink under an aura inchoate.

I am moaning for a hard-white
ergotamine pill
shored up with an opioid
it will trickle me to a place
of synaptic bliss.

The room sways as warmth
diffuses through my veins
my eyes flutter on a sigh.

The nausea is in retreat.
The room is afloat with joy and penitence.

Hallelujah!

On Night

I came across a copse of trees and stopped my breath

Fox Valley dreaming

The room is open
in expectation;
the Sunday paper
discarded on the table
waits patiently
beside the jar of chutney
but I pay them no attention
listening for the baby bats
that have not yet begun
their squawking,
my sleeping cheetahs
sprawled over the rug
soaking up the fire
as the washing folds
in the basket
and the night is winter.

Fox Valley night

The room is in awe
of the carnations;
they float on a perfume
that giddies the peaches
full and rose-coloured
with ripening.

Outside the window
the bats have begun
their Greek chorus.
I sip from my cup
you dip your whiskers
across my nose
in ticklish delicacy.
We listen to Mozart
your paw twitching
in the arc of my arm
our complicity
complete.

Leura night

I will not yet disturb
the embers
with another log
instead waiting
for the wind
shaking the veranda
to abate.
Earlier you showed me
the moon
full and hovering
over the power lines
holding a silent
street in a swoon
of longing.
Inside I set light
to another log
in slow combustion
the bolognese
still simmering
as you paired
your socks
absorbed
in a steady glow
of contemplation.

Leura moon

I had waited
for the hunter's moon to wax
entranced as it crept
across my room
like a shy visitor.

The room was waiting too
the masks hanging from a brick wall
blind with slow, pale lips
a shelf of wooden Buddhas
bent in wisdom over books,
the bowl a penitent bearer
of naughty figures
drawn and caught in frolic.

This sanguine moon
will be shaved to three quarters
in seven days
and continue through a cycle of crescent,
new moon and back to crescent again.

But only the hunter's moon
will arrive in this room
in all its suddenness
entering through an undrawn window
and I will make it feel at home.

Swinging in the rain

(after Gene Kelly)

My white leopard dashes
from a drenched bush
a snowy apparition.

Patting across
the wooden boards
in a swish of water
she digs into a log post
with a full scrape of paws.

Challenging me
with coal eyes
she waits for approbation
in a shake of fur.

My words of praise never fail her.

In a burst of spray
another summer storm in Leura
fades across the veranda.

Slowly I begin to dance
with a song in my throat
and a leopard
just dancing and swinging
in the rain.

Font

She brooded upon being and existence

This my Jug

I like it for its red belly,
the sobriety that emanates
from its consummate sense of self
honed over four millennia, balanced
between function and artistry
from the smoothness of high density plastic
to the spun clay of a ceramic pot.

Like a cocoon it exists in slow time
but it stands fast during the chatter of
table talk, the embodiment of pure water.
It receives compliments from dinner guests
over conversations on life and rent.
Nothing said will interrupt its flow,
its lip is always the apotheosis of dignity.

Meditating before it I feel astonished
by its beauty; a truth that is intrinsic to its art.
It leads me to its font –

                        and my jug runs over.

I give you flowers

I have heard there is a place
where women become flowers.
I have examined carefully
all the agapanthus in my garden –
there is a swath of purple ones
but I believe the white
would be a better bet.

I have inspected the bottlebrush
and stroked their feathery stamen
I have bemused my feline companions
who relish the opportunity
to shadow box between my knees.

I have knelt down to peel
a shroud of melaleuca
and peered up at a wisteria
savouring its delicate perfume.
I am reminded that women
are fond of perfume.

I have held my breath to see
a piccolo of brush turkey chicks
strutting down my garden path
in a line of lilting movement.
In that moment I was transfixed
for they wore the beauty of flowers.

The Fairest Font

The train on the Glacier Express
churned through the unconquerable mountains
of the wild Swiss Alps
stopping at a pretty village
for a short tourist break.
Wandering around
the graveside of the churchyard
we remarked on the neat formality
and the tender flowers, a devotion
of petals to each polished plaque.

I stepped into the nave
of a fourteenth-century church
drawn by a round porcelain bowl
balanced on a tripod.
My fingers slipped idly
in the smooth liquid of the font
brushing the faint cracks
of the bowl's edge, the dipped prints
that floated through centuries
of supplicant hands.

Moving closer to the surface of the water
I could see a mirror in a scar of light
on the bowl's mottled base.
Then I heard myself murmuring,
'Mirror of this sacred font
tell me if I am the fairest one
who has ever held your gaze.'

Guest house

(after Rumi)

This being human
is like a guest house
always open to a new arrival
turning up to dispute
whether the morning climate
is mild or inclement.

A crowd of dark thoughts
can appear angrily,
unexpected guests
can ring your doorbell
inviting your frustration
when you are peeling an orange
or even sitting on a bus.

Sometimes you can wake up
to a grimace of churlishness
the mysterious visitation
of feathers on your pillow
a pluck of meanness
a bag of depression
slightly damp from your breath.

It is best to let these in
and treat them like guests
find them comfortable chairs
offer them tea and cake.

If you smile graciously
suppressing your pique
they will soon drain their tea
and shuffle off with a promise -
to call in again.

Romance

I've always been attracted
to myth and fairy tale
it's the hopeless romantic
in me.

I relish the way
good and evil
are played out
in the human psyche;
evil in a fairy tale
can be such a subtle thing
a deeply sinuous coil
that winds its way
through our sleeping blood.

There is something about
the moral framework
of a fairy tale
the inhale of relief
that the proper order of things
has been restored,
that children have failed
to perish
in their stepmother's dark wood.

Mythology can be more brutal:
consider Medea's
cold-blooded killing
of her own children
a mind-stop of tragedy.

In a recent court case
a judge said
that he had difficulty
believing a woman
could murder her own child
because it did not make sense
that a mother
would do such a thing.

He clearly hadn't
dipped long enough
into myth and fairy tale;
they can be quite robust
in their pathology.

Pentagon

We were willing participants in her *noir* movie

Man of flowers

(vale john upton)

I watch him across
the table of wary writers
sharp-eyed
head hunched forward
his lizard tongue
waiting to garrotte
any member of the poetry group
who laid bare a quivering verb
or phrase;
he could light a bonfire
with our spooked adjectives
leaving blood on the table.

Then there was his death.

I remember him
sitting in the garden
wattle yellowing our table
his right eyebrow quizzically raised
under a navy beret.
He is talking about death
and how he misses his wife;
he says he can count the ways.
We smile and he tells me
that a good poem should have
the lightness of love.

I agree.

I am glad I could give him flowers.

Teddy bear

teddy bear teddy bear
turn around
teddy bear teddy bear
touch the ground

It was the teddy bear
lying across his dressing gown
on a double bed upstairs
that caught me.

There's no way
I could have missed it;
there it was
round brown eyes
in a large furry body
inert but cute
in a teddy bear sort of way.

My brother-in-law
was cuddling it.

He looked bemused as though
he wanted me to see him
and it was this assumption
of intimacy
that unsettled me.

As far as I'm concerned
whatever happens between
a man and his bear
should remain a secret.

Package

Packing is an art
I have never fully understood;
take the humble suitcase for example,
when packed
it encloses a whole personality
of style and geometric sensibility.

My brother-in-law,
a mathematician of the applied variety,
is a case in point.
I was intrigued
when he stayed overnight
with a surprisingly small suitcase
that was incongruent with his height.

After dinner I excused myself
and popped upstairs
to take a little peek inside
that very small suitcase.
Gently unzipping the flap
I could appreciate at once
the precision with which
it had been packed.

Each piece of clothing had been
tightly rolled and tucked,
most of the underwear neatly extended
to form a perimeter.

Two pocket handkerchiefs
folded into triangles
formed a square
one white with grey stripes
the other white with blue stripes.
A faded copy of *Playboy*
dated November 1986
was packed discreetly
between a shirt and a singlet.

Not bad for a man
with a serious passion –
for square-dancing.

The unkindest cut

It is taut in a way
I don't like
it is tight
in a way I too dislike;
it pulls muscle into a grimace
that looks like spite.

After one year
the injured nerve persists
causing pain to reverberate
through teeth, skin lip.
It stabs me when I chew
and even when I sit.

The bulge of surgery's rough
resides in half a mouth
and half a chin
frozen, with sensation
all mixed up.
I slumber sharp.

This doomed molar
was apparently too tough
for the man who dug and pulled
until he yanked it up.
A casual crime of blood and dentistry
that's mucked me up.

Lens

I am caught
in the eye's fleet blink

the flourish
of imaged light

the refraction
of sweet exchange

the osmosis
soft and aqueous:

But the eyes are yours
    Dr Shish

Circumstantial

Grace was a veil on a tree

Ode to a daughter

She manages
her smart Dior
business bag

She manages
her smooth mauve
shoulder bag
on matching
crisp-cut heels

She manages
the infinite buzz
of her life
as a harried lawyer
in Geneva

But wait –

She has mismanaged
my borrowed car keys.

She is just like me!

The wait

She sat opposite me
in the silence
of the waiting room
a full lid of life's fatigue
in the pouches of her eyes
the years draining into her fingers
that propped up her face
as if it were a flower
of crumpled petals.

She cradled her body
around the dress
that was complicit in her fatalism
for the X-rays would expose
the holes of resignation
in her bones.

The radiographer
walked into the room
and gently suggested
that she leave her handbag
with her husband.
There was a brief cross of irritation on her lips
but she relinquished it.

I held mine tight.

Wisp

The memory was on the table
she left it there
for me to see
she left her glass there too
with the last sip of her breath
but the words
the words were different –
she left those on the arm of her chair
the one I loved
so soft and mauve,
the colour of the spirit she said
the colour that may be too hidden to see.

She told me that one day this chair
the one I loved
would be mine –
those words I remember were light as air
as light as a prayer
folded with her love
for she knew I would find them there.

I scooped them up
with her address book
a clutch of memories in my hand
and a note that I folded away
to read –
perhaps on another day.

The art of passion

Whenever I hear
an exhortation
involving passion
as part of a moral compass
I feel a niggling concern.
'We are women
we can do anything'
goes one refrain
with a passionate punch
of the air.

Give me the good
old-fashioned passion
of hatred – within ethical limits
of course;
no cold dish this one
but vibrant with heat
disdain and exuberance.

Don't get me wrong;
passion has its place –
in fact, I would regard myself
as a reasonably passionate
woman.

The art of simplicity

(Inspired by Ivan Allbright)

Simplify me when I am dead
strip me of everything except
the morning song
that is my talisman
let me breathe deep
in the moisture of grass
that is green as a newborn day.

But do not confuse me with
the paradox of life's meaning
or even the beauty of a wandering star
for I had murder in my heart
when I last saw you –
gulping hatred with a crumpled face
and a grip of strangled hands.

In the end I went first:
my death – for most – an amusement
my eulogy – a sad farce
sprinkled on a coffin's head
a body draining
in a heart of darkness.

There was no lamentation
when I crossed the River Styx
hugging the white bones of my extinction
with the roar of dark blue water
in my ears –
but my last exhale was of bitter regret
that I had failed – desperately –
to murder you when I could.

Time for bed

Time is polyvalent –
>its mission statement flows endlessly

a vector moving us irreversibly
>forward.

We twist and turn and protest too much
>of time's inevitability

but like a cat sleeping in the sun
>it takes no notice.

Some of us devise intricately complex
>permutations and combinations
>>in order to pass time –

productively; they are called pure and applied –
>mathematicians.
>>Others are passionate about
>counting out their money

which is known as – greedy time.

To waste time can make us feel
>uncomfortably culpable
>>and even sinful.

In fact, it is better to peg up your clothes
>on a taut washing line

with a timer ticking in the basket
>if you are going
>>to pickle your time.

Time can be plucked or looped
    or flattened like an iron.
If you choose to balance your body
      on your hands
you may experience the lucidity of –
     yoga time.

  There is down time, party time
and kiss me quick on the lips time -
 there is time to put away childish things
    and be penitent time.

Then there is ambush time
    that whacks you on the side of your head
and the sometime slurpiness of chicken soup
     and toffee apple time.

There is the sensuousness of time
    that curls around poignant words
 and spindle-prick time that can make you sleep –

    For a hundred years.

Gradient of Love

In the quiet creek the wattle grows wild in mystery

Agapanthus Triptych

i.

The table is expectant
in the morning sun
a bowl brim-full of peaches
are sweet to my touch.
The agapanthus flowers
caught half in shadow
gleam in the vase
beside the bowl my coffee
warm in its cup.

ii.

The table is a spread
of simple contents
a slender cup hot with coffee
an agapanthus leaning in a vase
beside peaches
ripening in a bowl
their skin soft
in the afternoon haze.

iii.

On the table
the agapanthus flowers
drop from the vase
the bowl beside it
heavy with peaches.
I lift the cup to my lips
savouring its sweet taste
and close the door
slowly, behind me.

Lyric

My shadow self
calls to me
sweet and dark
from the wilderness
I cover myself with its shawl
and stalk the flat stones
in the dip of moonlight.

The trees murmur
swaying as they call me
in my lyric name
the pluck of the first words
of a melody that
sang to the moon.

In my kitchen
I can deconstruct
two-minute noodles
with a flick of the wrist.

In my parlour I slide
through the looking glass –

And frighten the air.

Still life

i.

The moonshine is sudden
on a midnight bush; it empties
a full cup of solemnity
in my arms, a bright ball
that fills up a night poignant
with dreams of wilderness.

ii.

My shadow is caught
in the moon's memory
it slides ghosting
between white gums;
I follow it down the track
and a sudden shower
sprinkles me with silver.

iii.

The night is slowly getting wet
as I ply my cloudy dreams
to a moon in still life.

Adoration on a Silent night

You snore upon my white pillow
as I touch the heave
of your warm belly
and marvel at the lightness of a paw
that lies so astonishingly
soft and limp in my hand.
Whiskers twitch
like distracted butterfly wings –
A leg hesitates to disturb the air.

An ear flicks in your sleep,
a breath moist from your nose
is gossamer to a mouth
that is tremulous in its secrecy.

I watch over you as your dream
is rounded by a little sigh.

Surely this is grace.

I count the angels.

Sunburnt Country

I love you as one loves most vulnerable things – urgently

Sunburnt Country

(after Dorothy Mckellar)

I woke in the middle of a night
to air that was dark
smouldering with ash
my breath barely a catch in a dream.

      I found you
         clinging
            to a tree on a dirt road
    singed, terrified,
  but alive and weeping.
    Fire bombs were exploding
        all around you.

The forest was a shriek of flames.

  I lifted you up
cradling you like a child
    in a nightmare
          holding you against
      the shudder of night
    singing you fiercely
        through lullabies and the desperation of love.

    Terror swept like wildfire across the country
        the sun a giant orb.

                Blood

  orange –
    menacing.

    Then suddenly: nothing.
  Almost nothing had survived
      animals were ripped apart – burnt, left for dead.
        Eucalypts shot up in flames
            seedlings – scorched spoilt, every one of them.

  The bush bled on the forest floor.

 There had once been birth
      there had once been rejoicing
      but this death
                 was the death of birth
            the wanton death –
      of the life
that had belonged to Earth.
        There would never be another forest here
          with the beauty of this one
              there would never be another forest here
              so beloved to species
                 so ecstatic in vast, pulsing habitat
                 so teeming in death.
      In the stillness later,
      eerily –
          the pop of bubbles.
                        In the crematoria –
                        the stench of death.
    There could be no more rejoicing
                    because all the songbooks
              were burnt.

There were evacuations by boat
    people fled choking towns
there was fighting, recrimination.

              I found you in embers
              on the beach, alive blinded by ash.
              I washed your eyes
              soothing your broken ear
              with a lullaby
              pulled from the sea.

The night was dark on the beach.
The waves were gentle,
the sea hummed.
We danced on the sand
under a pale, timeless moon.
              You were white,
              filled with salted stars
              as I carried you across the water.

        You left me
        with your tears.
    I promised you that I would never
        desert you
        never forsake you –
            Never.

In the middle of my life I dream of a solitary koala
watching me from the high branch of a gum tree.

Poetica

Flowers float lazily in my garden and water bubbles
in my dreams

To My Coy Mistress

written by Cleopatra R.
in dedication to Juliette (my *sine qua non*)

My distinct capacity to philosophise in the sun allows me to contemplate with anticipation the thisness of that dinner and the thatness of the next.

Ordinary cat food will never satisfy my existential need to wrestle with the amorphous nature of the cat bowl.

The ancient custom of mummifying my species has always been repugnant to me. As my lawyer, I expect you to prepare my will gratis.

I admire the Socratic method of cross-examination to achieve precise definitions. The question, what is beauty, is one I can easily answer.

The nature of love is another of my favourite dialectical questions. Nuzzling Juliette, I enjoy reciting *amo*, *amas*, *amat* amongst pristine laundry.

I was born in France and I speak French fluently. When I say *c'est la vie* I know exactly what it means.

My deep understanding of nihilism enables me to cope with angst when my mistress arrives home late. I am reminded of Nietzsche's 'that which does not destroy me makes me stronger'.

I like to practise the quietist techniques espoused by Lao-tzu when relaxing on the garden bench. They enable me to doze in an aura of unconditional acceptance.

When I look into the mirror I see the face of my sister. It provokes strange feelings of déjà vu.

I could never follow the extreme asceticism of Buddha as my bowl is always beckoning. But I can experience some degree of enlightenment on the last mouthful.

When a ball rolls under the table I retrieve it, aware that I am fulfilling five of Buddha's precepts: understanding, attention, action, mental control and clearness of thought. I should add livelihood as it is my noble duty to accommodate my mistress.

There are a few bite and scratch marks on my mistresses walnut table. She frequently asserts that my sister and I are naughty. Yet these scratchings if studied with intent, can reveal arcane patterns of geometry.

A box is a perfect place to meditate on the infinite absurdity of life: its awkward symmetry, its compactness and its sober predictability create a feeling of the hollowness of existence. If there is play it is a play of dignity, in the Buddhist sense, of course. My mistress will reliably emit squawks of laughter.

Symbiosis with your mistress facilitates the best understanding of primate psychology. They repay you with such touching gratitude.

My mistress never has to resort to massage or therapy. Stroking my soft fur for ten minutes with closed eyes almost always brings a long sigh of contentment. The curative powers of the cat have long been well documented.

Eternal optimists claim that life is just a bowl of cherries. They are wrong; the bowl is the container of the infinite.

It should be noted that my sister's apparent passivity is merely a mask for existential resignation. She acknowledges my superior nature; but we can both integrate complex desires while rolling in the sun.

It is said that the best milk is the milk of human kindness. I dispute this.

I admire the poetry of Emily Dickinson. I can relate to her adoration of the simple things in one's garden: the birds, the frogs, the insects and perhaps the small, secretive rodent. To find contentment in one's own garden is surely the singular gift of the cat. And there is always a stroll down the lane to break the existential monotony.

It should be known that I carry no baggage, I tread lightly on the earth and I am one with my shadow self. I will not be tricked by the counterfeit.

In my unique way I am devoted to my mistress. For the sake of congruity I am stoically prepared to sit on the lap of her partner. So in the last analysis, when all is said and done, when the thisness and thatness of life are resolved, when being becomes nothingness, when words turn to dust, when a star becomes a black hole, when ego is finally transcended, when the cat lies down with the lion, when the can opens with a turn of the screw, when conjecture becomes theorem and love occupies all of space and time… Oh, the Joycean delight of this tumble of thoughts! Roll over, Molly Bloom!

I challenge you not to look into my feline eyes and feel a sense of awe and sublimity. I am reminded of the Keatsian *Beauty is truth, truth is beauty*. To sum up, there is love, there is elegance and the ultimate cat.

I contemplate the arbitrary nature of life as I settle into my mistresses underwear drawer.

Aahhh, what coyness is this my mistress?

Existential dread? Some other time. I take no hostages.

(I graciously acknowledge discussions on primate psychology with my editor.)

Finis

My pocket was full of atoms

Saying it

You say
you dream about
the secret
of compressed time

I say
there is a place
where girls turn
into flowers

You say
you can stretch
complex groups
to infinity

I say
you can catch
a falling star
in your pocket

You say
how lucky
you are
to live with a poet

I say…

Notes

'Berry love': inspired by William Carlos Williams's poem 'This is just to say':

> I have eaten
> the plums
> that were in
> the icebox
>
> and which
> you were probably
> saving
> for breakfast
>
> forgive me
> they were delicious
> so sweet
> and so cold

'Swinging in the rain': 'Singing in the rain' was famously the centrepiece of a film starring Gene Kelly in 1952; he tap-danced and sang to this song while holding an umbrella and splashing through puddles.

'This my jug': the reference to beauty and truth is from Keats, 'Ode to a Grecian urn' – 'Beauty is truth, truth is beauty, – that is all ye know on earth, and all ye need to know'.

'The jug is the container of life – 'Meditating before it I feel astonished by its beauty / a truth that is intrinsic to its art.'

'My jug runs over' – from 'my cup runneth over' in the Hebrew Bible.

'I give you flowers': a flower has traditionally been used in Indian mythology as a symbol of women's generativity. In Sanskrit, a menstruating woman was called a woman in flower.

'The guesthouse': this poem is inspired by Jalaluddin Rumi's 'Guest house', in which he welcomes unexpected visitors such as joy, depression and meanness, as each has been sent as a guide from beyond.

'Romance': Medea is a figure from Greek mythology; she killed her children in cold blood to avenge the rejection of her husband Jason.

'Man of flowers': *Man of Flowers* is an Australian film directed by Paul Cox.

'He says he can count the ways' is after Elizabeth Barrett Browning's Sonnet 43, 'How Do I Love Thee / Let me count the ways'.

'Teddy bear': Teddy bear is from a nursery rhyme in which 'teddy bear teddy bear' is repeated as the first two lines throughout each refrain.

'The unkindest cut': the unkindest cut is a reference to one of the mythological quests that formed part of the ancient Greek Odyssey.

'The art of simplicity': this poem was inspired by Ivan Allbright's painting *The Picture of Dorian Gray*, from a novel of the same name by Oscar Wilde.

'Still life': 'The night is slowly getting wet' is from Lorca's 'Serenade, the night is getting wet…the night sings naked.'

'Adoration on a silent night': adoration as reverence for life.

'I count the angels' is an allusion to the Protestant mediaeval argument concerning how many angels can stand on the point of a pin.

'Sunburnt Country' is inspired by Dorothy McKellar's iconic poem 'Core of my heart', better known as 'I love a sunburnt country / a land of sweeping plains'. 'I love you as one loves most vulnerable things – urgently' are words from a sonnet by Craig Santos Perez. I wrote this poem in the wake of the horrific bushfires in Australia towards the end of 2019 and the beginning of 2020 that wiped out billions of native animals and destroyed ten million hectares, an area the size of the Netherlands. Fifty thousand koalas perished in the fires. The unprecedented droughts in Australia contributed to the ferocity of the fires, linked to record high temperatures as a result of global warming and the effects of climate change. 'Sunburnt Country' is a symbolic poem of tragedy, the tragedy of the death of a forest by fire. The view I express in this poem is that the Earth is a single living entity; its Nature is the bedrock of our being, of every form of life. This is what is sacred. Nature speaks through us of what it is to love madly, deeply and universally. To honour her, to articulate her grief, is what I have sought to do.

'To My Coy Mistress': the title is inspired by Andrew Marvell's 'To His Coy Mistress', an example of metaphysical poetry in the seventeenth century. It beguilingly begins with 'Had we but world enough, and time / this coyness, Lady were no crime.' The 'Roll over, Molly Bloom' stanza is a playful satire on the excessively long soliloquy of Molly Bloom, the female protagonist in James Joyce's *Ulysses*, published in 1922. *Sine qua non* – the Latin phrase 'that which is without' or 'above all things'. Existentialism – many of the phrases I use in 'To my coy mistress' are a pun on the language of existentialism, a philosophy that was substantially developed in France in the twentieth century. Jean-Paul Sartre and Simone de Beauvoir are its best known exponents. Exist- entialism had a considerable impact on Western thinking following World War I until the 1960s. It strongly influenced literature and even psychiatry and it contributed towards the pessimism of intellectual life, with concepts such as alienation, angst, nihilism, absurdity and existential dread entering mainstream vocabulary. Like many undergraduates in the 1960s, this author flirted with ideas of angst and alienation and the inherent absurdity of life. These concepts were enthusiastically taken up in Cleopatra's philosophising.

Cleopatra relieving the existential monotony of existence

www.ingramcontent.com/pod-product-compliance
Lightning Source LLC
Chambersburg PA
CBHW062142100526
44589CB00014B/1661